modern readers stage 3

Project Survival
MISSION 2

Eduardo Amos
Elisabeth Prescher

2nd edition

Richmond

© EDUARDO AMOS, ELISABETH PRESCHER, 2005

Richmond

Coordenação editorial: *Sandra Possas, Véra Regina A. Maselli*
Consultoria de língua inglesa: *Marylou Bielenstein*
Preparação do texto: *Margaret Presser*
Assistência editorial: *Gabriela Peixoto Vilanova*
Coordenação de produção gráfica: *André Monteiro, Maria de Lourdes Rodrigues*
Coordenação de revisão: *Estevam Vieira Lédo Jr.*
Revisão: *Elaine Cristina del Nero*
Edição de arte: *Claudiner Corrêa Filho*
Projeto gráfico de miolo e capa: *Ricardo Van Steen Comunicações e Propaganda Ltda./ Oliver Fuchs*
Ilustrações de miolo e capa: *Marcelo Martins*
Diagramação: *Tânia Balsini*
Coordenação de tratamento de imagens: *Américo Jesus*
Tratamento de imagens: *Fabio N. Precendo*
Saída de filmes: *Helio P. de Souza Filho, Marcio H. Kamoto*
Coordenação de produção industrial: *Wilson Aparecido Troque*

Impressão e acabamento: *Digital Page*

Dados Internacionais de Catalogação na Publicação (CIP)
(Câmara Brasileira do Livro, SP, Brasil)

Amos, Eduardo
    Project survival : mission 2 / Eduardo Amos,
Elisabeth Prescher. — 2. ed. —
São Paulo : Moderna, 2005. — (Modern readers ;
stage 3)

    1. Inglês (Ensino fundamental) I. Prescher,
Elisabeth. II. Título. III. Série.

04-8854   CDD-372.652

Índices para catálogo sistemático:
1. Inglês : Ensino fundamental 372.652

ISBN 85-16-04483-1

Reprodução proibida. Art. 184 do Código Penal e Lei 9.610 de 19 de fevereiro de 1998.

Todos os direitos reservados.

RICHMOND
EDITORA MODERNA LTDA.
Rua Padre Adelino, 758 — Belenzinho
São Paulo — SP — Brasil — CEP 03303-904
Central de atendimento ao usuário: 0800 771 8181
www.richmond.com.br
2013

Impresso no Brasil

Planet Earth sometime in the future.
Disagreement and ambition led the world to a nuclear war several decades ago.
Panic, sorrow, and radioactivity swept the planet.
Clouds of dust and hot, poisonous air covered everything.
No plant, no insect, no bird, no animal survived.
Life vanished from the surface of the "blue planet".

Under the surface, however, six people in a nuclear shelter survived the holocaust.

The shelter was part of a secret plan called Project Survival. The idea of the project was to save the human race from extinction in case of a nuclear war.

The first days, time went by very slowly for the six people in the shelter. All they had to do was wait — wait and hope.

Hope that the leaders of the world would come to an agreement. Hope that they could soon leave the shelter.

They listened to the radio and watched TV very anxiously those days. But the news from the world above was more terrifying each day.

Then one day the radio and television were silenced. From that moment on they knew they were probably the only living people on earth.

Everything was difficult in the beginning. They had to learn how to live in the limited space of the shelter. They had to overcome racial, religious, and language differences. They had to build a community.

Time passed. Babies were born and the community grew. The elders taught the youngsters. Work was shared by everyone.

The children learned languages, music, arts, crafts, computer engineering, and sports. They were happy. Video tapes and computer screens helped the young people learn about the civilization of their ancestors. The elders spent hours telling stories about the world outside.

The community lived in peace and harmony.

After many years, however, they all started to share a feeling of incompleteness. The elders missed the sunshine, the summer breezes, and the scent of flowers. The youngsters were anxious to see for themselves the things they knew only through videos.

April 21st. Year 40.

The whole community was gathered for a special assembly. Orak, the leader, was speaking.

"Forty years ago, six people — our elders — entered this shelter. Their mission was to start a new civilization." He paused, looked around, and continued. "And here we are now! According to the instructions they received at that time, this community should attempt to contact the outside world forty years after the holocaust. That's what we are going to do in a few days."

Everybody reacted to the news enthusiastically. Orak continued.

"Our scientists are also very anxious to open the shelter. Besides, our community is growing fast and in a few years it will be too small for all of us."

"We want to go out!" said a boy.

"Yes, let's open the doors!" shouted another.

The leader raised his hands to calm down the crowd. "That's what we all want, my friends. But it isn't so simple. This shelter was built in a valley, and we don't know the exact effects of the war on this area. We don't know what the world is like now. Is there life up there? What kind of life?"

While Orak was speaking, enthusiasm gradually disappeared. He then talked about the investigative mission they were going to send to the surface. The purpose of the mission was to check living conditions outside the shelter. The community was going to make a decision based on the information collected by the explorers.

"In a few days a team of explorers will leave the shelter for an hour. It can be very dangerous. We need five volunteers. There's only one restriction: children and scientists cannot volunteer. Anyone who is interested, please, come to my office in the next twenty-four hours. That's all for today. This meeting is over."

First day of training. Hour 7.

When the door of the Training Center opened, a thirty-eight-year-old man walked in. He was one of the most respected scientists in the community. The five volunteers were waiting for him: elder Primus, one of the six people that had founded the community; Simon, 30 years old; Bella, 28; Tory, 18; and Lena, 19.

"Good morning, Dr. Ellstrung!" greeted the volunteers.

"Good morning, my friends," answered the scientist.

"We're glad to be here and to have you as our instructor," said Tory. Ellstrung smiled and said, "I am glad you're here! This is a very important moment for me. I belong to the first generation. I was one of the first babies born in the shelter, and one of the first scientists too. I love this place. Project Survival is my life, my home, and my prison... our prison."

"That's why we're here, Dr. Ellstrung," said Bella.

"Yes, we want to help our community find its way to freedom," added Simon.

The scientist told them about the possible perils they were going to face. "This is more dangerous than you can imagine. First of all, nobody knows the level of radiation outside. We don't know if our special suits will protect you well enough."

The volunteers listened silently. Ellstrung continued. "Second, if there is life outside, what kind of life can it be? What are you going to find? Plants? Animals?... Mutant creatures? Monsters?... We aren't sure of anything!... There's much we can do for you in here, but

there's little we can do when you're outside."

Ellstrung stopped. Then he looked at each member of the group and said, "You know that you'll risk your lives. If you want to change your mind you have to tell me now. This is your last chance to quit."

The room remained silent.

Ellstrung took the team to another room.
"These are the suits you're going to wear. As you can see, they are very light. Even so, my colleagues and I believe that you're going to feel very tired on the surface."

"Why?" asked Simon.

"Because this is the first time you're going to walk at ground level. Also, you'll be exposed to real sunlight for a long time. Finally, you may find severe environmental conditions," explained Ellstrung. "Therefore, each of you will carry only one piece of equipment. Simon will carry the oxygen tanks. Elder Primus will be in charge of the communication equipment, and Tory will operate the Geiger counter. Lena and Bella will take a camera and bags to record and collect samples of soil material and living organisms."

Then the team examined the suits and equipment.

"Look at them very carefully. Touch them," said Ellstrung.

"What are these?" asked Bella, pointing at some strong thin tubes connecting one suit to the other. "What are they for?"

"They'll be your umbilical cords," answered Ellstrung. "Your lives will depend on them. These tubes will supply you with oxygen from the tanks."

Elder Primus looked closely at the tubes. Then he turned to the scientist. "You mean we'll have to walk close together?"

"Yes," said Ellstrung. "You'll have to stay together all the time. Each tube is five meters long. So, that's how far from each other you can be. Whatever you decide to do and wherever you decide to go, the whole team must follow."

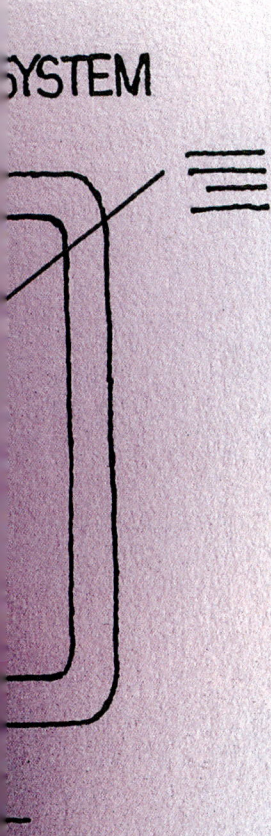

Last day of training. Hour 21.

There was only one way to get out of the shelter — through the isolation chambers. There were four chambers and each chamber had two air locks. The team had to learn how the system worked.

"You'll have to open the first air lock, enter the chamber, and close the air lock," explained Ellstrung. "Don't walk to the second air lock before closing the first. This is the way you'll move from chamber to chamber. You'll have one and a half hour of oxygen from the moment you enter the first chamber. We believe you'll be able to go through the chambers in less than thirty minutes. So, you'll have about one hour to stay outside. The last air lock will remain open for one hour. Then it'll automatically close."

Ellstrung also said that there was a password to open each air lock. "There's a keyboard on each door. Type the password on the keyboard and press the OPEN button."

"But what will happen if there's a failure in the locking system? You must remember that this is the first time the system is going to be operated in forty years," said Simon.

"In case of failure, it's possible to open the locks manually. Here is a diagram showing how to do it," Ellstrung said. "The problem is that the manual operation takes time. That means you'll have less time to be outside."

The great day came.

At hour 10, scientists and the elders were in the Security Room to wish the explorers good luck.

Elder Primus and the other volunteers were in front of the first air lock. They were ready to go. Their hearts beat fast as they put their helmets on and activated the system.

They entered the first chamber and closed the first air lock. They were on their own.

They walked to the second air lock and typed the password. The door opened.

They crossed three chambers without problem, but when they reached the air lock to the last chamber, the system failed. The air lock to the last chamber didn't open.

Simon and Tory had to open the air lock manually.

When they got to the last air lock, elder Primus typed in the last password. The chamber opened.

Bright sunlight filled the chamber.

Tears rolled down elder Primus's face as he looked outside. "This is the earth, my children," he said.

The others were speechless. They took a few steps outside. Green grass surrounded them. There were flowers, bushes, and small trees covering the valley. But there was no sign of monsters or any living creatures.

They heard Ellstrung over the radio.

"Hello! Can you hear me? What's going on? Are you all right? Answer, please!!!"

"It's springtime!" said elder Primus calmly. Then he described everything he could see.

"It's wonderful up here, Dr. Ellstrung!" shouted Tory. "There's life and the levels of radiation are low. I believe everything is okay."

"I'm not sure about that," protested Simon. "There's plant life, but I can't see any birds or insects. There's no animal life around here!"

"Elder Primus!" called Ellstrung over the radio. "That's strange. What do you think of it?"

"Simon is right," said elder Primus. "We can't see any sign of animal life here. But...  Project Survival was built in a valley surrounded by hills. Maybe we can find something else beyond the hills."

"Why don't we walk up the hill then?" asked Bella.

"That's exactly what I wanted to do," said elder Primus enthusiastically. "I remember there was a lake north of the valley."

Lena was reluctant. "A walk up the hill may be too risky. And I don't think we have enough time."

"We aren't going up the hill!" protested Simon. "Let's do what we're supposed to do — walk around the shelter, collect samples, and go back at the right time."

"But Simon," said Tory. "The community depends on us to make a careful decision and we may not have enough information."

"Let's walk up!" shouted Bella.

"Yes, let's!" agreed elder Primus. "Let's see what's beyond the hill."

Simon looked puzzled. "What does the community say?" he asked.

"We really need more information," answered Ellstrung. "But it's risky. You'll have to decide by yourselves... But do it quickly. You have only forty-five minutes left."

# The Situation

Project Survival is a community that lives in a nuclear shelter. It is time to explore the outside world and see if they can safely leave the shelter.

A group of volunteers is sent to the surface. The information they gather near the shelter may not be enough.

The only way to get more information is to walk up the hill. But they have only forty-five minutes of oxygen left. The group has to decide. Will they go back safely but without the necessary information? Will they risk their lives and walk up the hill?

Now you are one of the volunteers on the team: Simon, Lena, Bella, Tory, or elder Primus. Discuss the situation with your group and decide what to do. Then make a report.

REPORT

We decide to _____

because _____

_____
_____
_____
_____
_____
_____
_____

(Your name)

 **What I saw on the surface**
(Draw or make an artwork. Use your imagination.)

Come, my friends,
It's not too late to seek a newer world.
For my purpose holds to sail beyond the sunset.
And though we are not now that strength
Which in old days moved earth and heaven,
That which we are, we are;
One equal temper of heroic hearts,
Made weak by time and fate,
But strong in will
To strive, to seek, to find, and not to yield.

(Tennyson, **Ulysses**. Adapted version.)

KEY WORDS

The meaning of each word corresponds to its use in the context of the story (see page number 00)

a few (8) alguns
above (5) acima
according to (8) de acordo com
activate (16) ativar
add (10) acrescentar
ago (3) atrás
agree (20) concordar
agreement (5) acordo
air (3) ar
air lock (15) câmara de compressão
ambition (3) ambição
ancestor (7) ancestral
another (8) outro
anxious (7) ansioso
anxiously (5) ansiosamente
anything (10) algo; nada
as (10) como; quando
beat (16) bater, pulsar
because (12) porque
beginning (6) início
believe (12) acreditar
belong (10) pertencer
besides (8) além de
beyond (20) além
bird (3) pássaro
breeze (7) brisa
bright (18) brilhante
build (6) construir
bush (18) arbusto
button (15) botão
calm down (9) acalmar
carefully (13) cuidadosamente

carry (12) carregar
case (15) caso
check (9) verificar
closely (13) (de) perto
cloud (3) nuvem
come (6) vir
condition (9) condição
connect (13) conectar
contact (8) contactar
could (19) poderia
cover (3) cobrir
craft (7) ofício
creature (10) criatura
crowd (9) multidão
dangerous (9) perigoso
decade (3) década
decide (13) decidir
depend (13) depender
describe (19) descrever
difficult (6) difícil
disagreement (3) desacordo
discuss (21) discutir
each (11) cada
earth (3) terra
elder (6) mais velho
else (20) mais
enough (10) suficiente
enthusiastically (8) entusiasticamente
environmental (12) ambiental
everyone (16) todos
everything (3) tudo
explain (12) explicar

expose (12) expor
extinction (4) extinção
failure (15) falha
fast (8) rápido
fate (24) destino
feel (12) sentir
feeling (7) sentimento
few (8) poucos
fill (18) encher
find (10) achar
follow (13) seguir
freedom (10) liberdade
gather (8) reunir
Geiger counter (12) contador Geiger
glad (10) alegre
go back (20) voltar
go out (18) sair
greet (10) saudar
ground (12) chão
grow (8) crescer
happen (15) acontecer
hear (18) ouvir
heart (16) coração
heaven (24) céu
helmet (16) capacete
hill (20) colina
hope (4) esperar
hot (3) quente
however (7) entretanto
idea (4) idéia
in charge of (12) encarregado de
insect (3) inseto
keyboard (15) teclado
kind (9) tipo
know (9) saber
lake (20) lago
last (11) último
leader (8) líder
learn (6) aprender
leave (9) partir
level (10) nível

life (3) vida
listen (10) escutar
little (10) pouco
live (6) viver
locking system (15) sistema de fechamento
low (19) baixo
may (12) poder
maybe (20) talvez
mean (13) significar; querer dizer
miss (7) sentir saudade
monster (10) monstro
mutant (10) mutante
need (9) precisar
news (8) notícia
nobody (10) ninguém
north (20) norte
outside (7) do lado de fora
overcome (6) superar
panic (3) pânico
part (4) parte
password (15) senha
people (7) pessoas, povo
peril (10) perigo
piece (12) peça
plan (4) plano
planet (3) planeta
poisonous (3) venenoso
probably (5) provavelmente
project (10) projeto
purpose (9) propósito
puzzled (20) confuso
quickly (20) rapidamente
quit (11) desistir
radioactivity (3) radioatividade
raise (9) levantar
reach (17) alcançar
react (8) reagir
ready (16) pronto
receive (8) receber
reluctant (20) relutante
remain (11) permanecer

report (21) relatar; relatório
restriction (9) restrição
risky (20) arriscado
safely (21) cautelosamente
sample (12) amostra
save (4) salvar
scent (7) odor
screen (7) tela
secret (4) secreto; segredo
seek (24) procurar
several (3) vários
severe (12) difícil, árduo
share (6) repartir, compartilhar
shelter (6) abrigo
should (8) deveria
shout (8) gritar
sign (18) sinal
slowly (4) vagarosamente
smile (10) sorrir
so (9) então
soil (12) solo
something (20) algo
sometime (3) algum tempo
soon (5) logo
sorrow (3) tristeza
speechless (18) sem palavras
spend (7) gastar, passar
springtime (19) primavera
start (7) começar
stay (13) permanecer
step (18) passo
strange (20) estranho
strength (24) força
strive (24) lutar
suit (10) traje
summer (7) verão
sunlight (12) luz do sol
sunshine (7) brilho do sol
supply (13) suprimento; suprir
sure (10) certo
surface (3) superfície
surround (18) rodear

survival (10) sobrevivência
survive (10) sobreviver
sweep (3) varrer
terrifying (5) aterrorizante
then (9) então
team (9) time
tear (18) lágrima
tell (7) contar
therefore (12) portanto
thing (7) coisa
those (5) aqueles
through (7) através
together (13) juntos
too (8) também; demais
touch (13) toque; tocar
tube (13) tubo
turn (13) vez; virar
type (15) digitar
under (4) sob
valley (9) vale
vanish (3) desaparecer
wait (10) esperar
want (8) querer
war (3) guerra
watch (5) observar, ver
wear (12) vestir, usar
whatever (13) o que quer que
wherever (13) onde quer que
while (9) enquanto
whole (8) todo, total
will (8) desejo
wish (16) desejo; desejar
without (17) sem
world (3) mundo
yield (24) ceder
youngster (6) jovem

Expressions

Change one's mind (11) Mudar de idéia
even so (12) mesmo assim

ACTIVITIES

Vocabulary exercises

A. Find the opposites.

1. disagreement
2. under
3. save
4. open
5. outside
6. beginning
7. leave
8. light
9. difficult
10. future

( ) above
( ) arrive
( ) past
( ) close
( ) heavy
( ) agreement
( ) easy
( ) inside
( ) destroy
( ) end

B. Find the synonyms.

1. share
2. several
3. kind
4. start
5. happy
6. tell
7. vanish
8. check
9. purpose
10. project

( ) type
( ) say
( ) verify
( ) disappear
( ) goal
( ) divide
( ) begin
( ) glad
( ) many
( ) plan

C. Fill in with the correct preposition.

| at | on | with | about | into | to |

1. All the students were anxious _____ the oral test.
2. We are going to make a project based _____ his idea.

3. She said she didn't want to talk _____ her private life.
4. Young people usually depend _____ their parents to live.
5. That river is going to supply us _____ water.
6. Her sorrow turned _____ happiness when she saw him.
7. He looked _____ the valley and cried.
8. They will be exposed _____ sunlight for the first time.
9. How is he going to react _____ the news?
10. We are going to learn _____ the new locking system.

D. Choose the best word for each blank.

> hope   surface
> feeling   password   sample
> wait   ancestors
> wherever   failure   overcome

1. I'm going to follow you _____ you go.
2. We shared a _____ of discomfort after he entered the room.
3. Can you bring me a _____ of the new product?
4. They are going to _____ for you at the bus stop.
5. The boy couldn't enter the system because he didn't know the _____.
6. Where are your _____ from?
7. We _____ we can come to an agreement.
8. You get stronger when you _____ difficulties.
9. If there is a _____ in the system, call me.
10. I'm going to meet the group under the _____.

Comprehension exercises

E. Choose the correct alternative.

1. What led the world to a nuclear war?

   a) Panic, sorrow, and radioactivity.
   b) Disagreement and ambition.
   c) Clouds of dust and poisonous air.

2. Six people survived the holocaust

   a) in a shelter under the surface.
   b) because they were watching TV.
   c) because war was not declared.

3. They knew they were the only living people on earth

   a) because the news from the world above was terrifying.
   b) when the radio and television were silenced.
   c) because the leaders of the world didn't come to an agreement.

4. In the beginning everything was difficult in the shelter because

   a) there were many babies.
   b) there was a feeling of incompleteness.
   c) they had to build a community.

5. The community was going to send an investigative mission

   a) to live in the valley.
   b) to calm down the crowd.
   c) to find out about living conditions on the surface.

6. Dr. Ellstrung

   a) was one of the elders.
   b) was born in the shelter.
   c) wasn't born in the shelter.

7. It was dangerous to open the shelter because

   a) nobody knew what they were going to find on the surface.
   b) there were mutant creatures on the surface.
   c) the levels of radiation on the surface were high.

8. The "umbilical cords"

   a) were going to supply the new babies with oxygen.
   b) were going to supply the volunteers with oxygen from the tanks.
   c) connected one bottle of oxygen to another.

9. The explorers had to walk together because

   a) it was dangerous to walk alone on the surface.
   b) nobody was sure of anything.
   c) the suits were connected by tubes.

10. In case of failure in the locking system,

    a) they were going to die in the chamber.
    b) they were going to ask for help.
    c) it was possible to open the locks manually.